INVESTMENT

WHAT YOU MUST KNOW TO BE A GREAT INVESTOR

BY

JACK ELON

TABLE OF CONTENTS

WHERE NOT TO INVEST

WHO TO MANAGE INVESTMENT

WHO TO PARTNER WITH IN INVESTMENT

RISKS ASSOCIATED WITH INVESTMENT

HOW TO SAFEGUARD YOUR INVESTMENT

20 LAWS OF INVESTMENT

HOW TO PLAN INVESTMENT

HOW TO SOURCE FOR CAPITAL FOR INVESTMENT

31 SECTORS TO TRY INVESTMENT

INVESTMENT

Investment refers to the act of allocating money, resources, or capital to acquire an asset, venture, or financial instrument with the expectation of generating income, appreciation, or a return on investment over time. It involves committing funds to earn a profit or achieve specific financial goals.

Investing is a popular way to grow wealth and achieve financial goals. However, the best investment strategy depends on several factors such as your financial situation, risk tolerance, investment goals, and time horizon.

Investment can take various forms, including:

Financial investments: This category includes investing in stocks, bonds, mutual funds, ETFs, options, futures, and other securities or financial instruments traded in various markets.

Real estate investments: This involves purchasing properties, such as residential or commercial real estate, land, or real estate investment trusts (REITs) to earn rental income or capital appreciation.

Business investments: Investing in businesses can involve providing capital to start or expand a business, acquiring ownership stakes in private companies, or investing in publicly traded companies' shares.

Commodities investments: Commodities like gold, oil, natural gas, agricultural products, or other raw materials can be invested directly or through commodity-focused investment vehicles.

Alternative investments: These are non-traditional investments that fall outside the realm of stocks, bonds, and real estate. They can include investments in private equity, venture capital, hedge funds, art, collectibles, cryptocurrencies, and more.

The primary goal of investment is to generate a return on the invested capital. This return can come in the form of capital appreciation (an increase in the value of the investment), income (such as dividends, interest, or rental payments), or a combination of both. Investors assess various factors, including risk tolerance, expected returns, liquidity, and investment time horizon when choosing their investment options.

It's important to note that investments carry risks, and returns are not guaranteed. The value of investments can fluctuate based on market conditions, economic factors, and individual performance. Investors should carefully evaluate investment opportunities, conduct thorough research, and consider diversifying their portfolios to manage risks effectively. Seeking advice from financial professionals can provide additional guidance tailored to individual circumstances and investment goals.

Here are some general investment options and strategies that you can consider:

Stock market: Investing in individual stocks or exchange-traded funds (ETFs) can provide opportunities for capital appreciation. Research and choose companies or sectors that align with your investment goals. Consider diversifying your portfolio to reduce risk.

Bonds: Bonds are debt securities issued by governments or corporations. They offer fixed interest payments over a specific period, making them relatively less risky than stocks. Bonds can provide stability and income generation in a portfolio.

Mutual funds: Mutual funds pool money from multiple investors to invest in a diversified portfolio of stocks, bonds, or other assets. They are managed by professionals, making them suitable for investors who prefer a hands-off approach.

Real estate: Investing in real estate can offer both income and potential appreciation. You can purchase properties for rental income or invest in real estate investment trusts (REITs), which are companies that own and manage income-generating real estate.

Index funds: Index funds are a type of mutual fund or ETF that aims to replicate the performance of a specific market index, such as the S&P 500. They provide broad market exposure and are often recommended for long-term investors due to their low fees and passive management.

Diversification: Spreading your investments across different asset classes and sectors can help reduce risk. Diversification can be achieved through a combination of stocks, bonds, real estate, and other investment vehicles.

Dollar-cost averaging: This strategy involves investing a fixed amount of money at regular intervals, regardless of market conditions. By consistently investing over time, you can benefit from the fluctuations in the market and potentially reduce the impact of market timing.

Retirement accounts: Contributing to retirement accounts such as 401(k)s or IRAs can provide tax advantages and help build long-term wealth. Take advantage of employer-matching contributions and consider maximizing your contributions if possible.

Education savings accounts: If you have children, consider investing in education savings accounts like 529 plans. These accounts offer tax advantages for saving for education expenses.

Consult a financial advisor: If you are unsure about investing or need personalized advice, consider consulting a financial advisor who can assess your situation and recommend appropriate investment strategies.

Remember, investing involves risk, and it's important to do thorough research, understand your goals, and consider your risk tolerance before making any investment decisions.

20 DEFINITIONS OF THE CONCEPT OF INVESTMENT

Investment refers to the act of allocating money, resources, or capital to a project, business, or financial instrument with the expectation of generating income or profit over time.

Investment is the process of purchasing assets such as stocks, bonds, real estate, or commodities to earn a return on the invested capital.

Investment involves making a conscious decision to save and allocate funds to achieve long-term financial goals and increase wealth.

Investment is the act of committing money or resources to a venture or opportunity to gain potential financial returns or benefits.

Investment refers to the acquisition of assets or securities to generate income through dividends, interest, rent, or capital appreciation.

Investment involves setting aside funds or resources to engage in productive or income-generating activities, with the expectation of future financial rewards.

Investment is the deliberate deployment of funds into different financial instruments or assets to achieve financial growth or preserve wealth.

Investment is the act of putting money into a specific project, business, or financial vehicle in anticipation of earning a positive return on the initial capital.

Investment is a strategic decision to allocate financial resources to participate in economic activities that have the potential to generate profits or increase value.

Investment is the process of exchanging money or assets for securities, properties, or other financial instruments to generate income or appreciation.

Investment refers to the act of buying, holding, or trading financial instruments or assets to generate wealth, build assets, or secure future financial stability.

Investment involves the commitment of financial resources or capital with the expectation of achieving capital gains, income, or other financial benefits over a specified period.

Investment is the act of placing money, time, or effort into an enterprise, venture, or asset class to gain a return or profit.

Investment is the process of making informed decisions to allocate funds or resources to difftot investment options or opportunities, aiming to maximize returns while managing risks.

Investment refers to the act of converting savings or surplus funds into assets, properties, or financial instruments to generate income or appreciation over time.

Investment is the practice of purchasing financial securities, shares, or assets to capitalize on market opportunities and earn a positive return on investment.

Investment involves the commitment of resources into various financial instruments or projects, based on careful analysis and evaluation of potential risks and rewards.

Investment is the act of entrusting capital or funds into different avenues or assets with the expectation of obtaining financial gains or benefits in the future.

Investment is the deliberate act of placing money or assets into ventures, businesses, or financial products to achieve long-term financial goals or objectives.

Investment involves the process of allocating financial resources to acquire assets or securities to preserve or increase the value of the invested capital.

UNDERSTANDING SHORT-TERM INVESTMENTS

Short-term investments are financial assets that are held for a relatively brief period, typically ranging from a few days to a few years. Unlike long-term investments, which are intended to be held for an extended period, short-term investments are focused on generating returns over a shorter time frame. The meaning of short-time investment can vary depending on the context, but in general, it refers to investment strategies that prioritize liquidity, quick returns, and lower risk compared to long-term investment options. In this section, we will delve deeper into the meaning of short-term investments and explore their key characteristics and benefits.

Liquidity: One of the primary advantages of short-term investments is their high level of liquidity. These investments can be easily converted into cash without significant loss of value. This is crucial for investors who may need quick access to funds for emergencies or other financial obligations. Examples of liquid short-term investments include money market accounts, Treasury bills, and certificates of deposit.

Low risk: Short-term investments often involve lower levels of risk compared to long-term investments. While all investments carry some degree of risk, short-term investments are typically less exposed to market volatility and economic fluctuations. The shorter time frame mitigates the impact of unforeseen events and allows investors to adjust their strategies more quickly. Conservative short-term investment options include high-quality corporate bonds and short-term government securities.

Quick returns: Short-term investments are designed to provide relatively fast returns on investment. They aim to generate income or capital gains over a shorter period compared to long-term investments, where returns may take several years or even decades to materialize. This characteristic makes short-term investments appealing to individuals or organizations seeking to maximize their returns within a limited time frame.

Diversification: Short-term investments can be an integral part of a well-diversified investment portfolio. By including a mix of short-term and long-term investments, investors can balance risk and return. Short-term investments can provide stability and liquidity, while long-term investments offer the potential for higher returns over an extended period. This diversification strategy helps manage risk and optimize overall portfolio performance.

Examples of short-term investments: There are various types of short-term investments available to investors, depending on their risk tolerance, investment goals, and time horizon. Some common examples include money market funds, short-term bonds, Treasury bills, commercial paper, and bank savings accounts. These investment vehicles offer different levels of risk and return, allowing investors to choose the option that aligns with their specific requirements.

Considerations and Risks of Short-Term Investments

While short-term investments offer certain advantages, it is essential to be aware of the considerations and risks associated with this investment approach. Understanding these factors can help investors make informed decisions and manage their expectations effectively.

Lower potential returns: Short-term investments generally yield lower returns compared to long-term investments. The emphasis on stability and liquidity often means sacrificing the potential for higher growth. Investors seeking substantial long-term capital appreciation may need to consider longer investment horizons or explore other investment avenues.

Interest rate risk: Short-term investments, particularly fixed-income securities, are susceptible to interest rate fluctuations. When interest rates rise, the value of existing fixed-income investments may decline. This risk is particularly relevant for bondholders, as the market value of bonds with fixed coupon rates decreases when newer bonds with higher yields enter the market. Monitoring interest rate trends is essential for short-term investors to adjust their strategies accordingly.

Inflation risk: Inflation erodes the purchasing power of money over time. Short-term investments with low returns may not keep pace with inflation, resulting in a loss of real value. Investors must consider the potential impact of inflation on their short-term investments and evaluate whether the returns generated will be sufficient

UNDERSTANDING LONG-TERM INVESTMENTS

Long-term investments are a crucial aspect of financial planning that individuals, businesses, and institutions undertake to achieve their financial goals over an extended period. Unlike short-term investments, which focus on immediate gains, long-term investments are designed to provide financial security and growth over an extended timeframe, typically spanning several years or even decades. This concept revolves around the idea of allocating funds to assets that have the potential to appreciate significantly over time, thereby generating substantial returns. In this article, we will explore the key characteristics, benefits, and considerations associated with long-term investments.

Characteristics of Long-Term Investments

Time Horizon: The primary characteristic of long-term investments is the extended time horizon over which they are held. Investors commit their capital to various financial instruments, such as stocks, bonds, real estate, or mutual funds, with the understanding that these investments will yield returns over a more extended period. This longer time frame allows for the potential to ride out short-term fluctuations and benefit from compounding returns.

Potential for Higher Returns: Long-term investments offer the potential for higher returns compared to short-term investments. By investing in assets that have historically demonstrated growth over time, investors can benefit from the power of compounding. This means that the returns generated on the initial investment are reinvested and can generate additional returns, creating a snowball effect that can significantly increase the overall return on investment.

Diversification: Long-term investment strategies often emphasize diversification. By spreading investments across different asset classes, industries, or geographical regions, investors can mitigate risk and protect their portfolios from significant losses. Diversification helps ensure that if one investment underperforms, gains from other investments can potentially offset the losses, resulting in a more stable and consistent return.

Benefits of Long-Term Investments

Wealth Accumulation: Long-term investments provide individuals with the opportunity to accumulate wealth gradually over time. By consistently investing a portion of their income into a well-diversified portfolio, investors can benefit from the compounding effect and generate substantial wealth in the long run. This wealth accumulation can be instrumental in achieving financial goals such as retirement planning, education funding, or major life milestones.

Capital Appreciation: Many long-term investments, such as stocks and real estate, have the potential to appreciate significantly over time. By investing in assets that align with growth industries, emerging markets, or undervalued sectors, investors can benefit from capital appreciation. This growth in asset value can generate substantial returns when the investments are eventually sold or liquidated.

Income Generation: Long-term investments can also provide a regular stream of income. Dividend-paying stocks, bonds, rental properties, or interest-bearing accounts can generate passive income for investors, enhancing their overall financial stability. This income can be reinvested to further accelerate wealth accumulation or be used to cover expenses and enhance one's standard of living.

Considerations for Long-Term Investments

Risk Tolerance: Long-term investments are not immune to risk. Market volatility, economic downturns, and other factors can impact the value of investments over time. Investors need to assess their risk tolerance and select investments that align with their comfort level. Higher-risk investments may offer the potential for greater returns but also carry a higher probability of losses.

Research and Due Diligence: Engaging in thorough research and due diligence is crucial before committing to long-term investments. Understanding the fundamentals of the investment, evaluating the historical performance, analyzing market trends, and seeking professional advice are essential steps in making informed investment decisions. The more information an investor gathers, the better equipped they are to make sound choices.

BENEFITS OF INVESTMENT

Investing can offer numerous benefits that can help individuals grow their wealth, achieve financial goals, and secure their future. Here are some key benefits of investment:

Wealth accumulation: Investing allows individuals to potentially grow their wealth over time. By allocating funds to various investment vehicles such as stocks, bonds, real estate, or mutual funds, investors have the opportunity to generate returns that exceed inflation and increase their overall net worth.

Income generation: Many investment options provide regular income in the form of dividends, interest, or rental payments. Investments such as dividend-paying stocks, bonds, or real estate can offer a steady stream of income, which can supplement salary or other sources of revenue.

Capital appreciation: Investments in assets like stocks or real estate have the potential for capital appreciation. As the value of these assets increases over time, investors can benefit from the appreciation and sell their investments at a profit if desired.

Diversification: Investing allows individuals to diversify their portfolios by spreading their investments across different asset classes, sectors, or geographical regions. Diversification helps reduce the risk associated with holding a single investment and can enhance the overall risk-adjusted returns.

Inflation protection: Investing can provide a hedge against inflation. Inflation erodes the purchasing power of money over time, but investments that outpace inflation can help maintain and increase the real value of wealth.

Retirement planning: Investing is a crucial component of retirement planning. By investing in retirement accounts like 401(k)s or IRAs, individuals can accumulate funds over time to support their retirement lifestyle and ensure financial security during their non-working years.

Tax advantages: Certain investment vehicles offer tax advantages. Retirement accounts, such as IRAs and 401(k)s, can provide tax deductions or tax-free growth, allowing investors to reduce their tax liability and optimize their overall financial situation.

Portfolio customization: Investing allows individuals to tailor their portfolios to their specific goals, risk tolerance, and preferences. Investors can choose from a wide range of investment options and strategies to build a portfolio that aligns with their financial objectives and values.

Financial independence: Successful investing can lead to financial independence, where individuals have accumulated enough wealth to sustain their desired lifestyle without relying solely on income from employment. This freedom provides greater flexibility and peace of mind.

Legacy planning: Investments can be passed on to future generations as part of an estate plan, allowing individuals to leave a financial legacy for their loved ones or charitable causes.

It's important to note that investing carries risks, and there are no guarantees of returns. Individuals should carefully evaluate their financial situation, goals, and risk tolerance before making investment decisions. Consulting with a financial advisor can provide personalized guidance based on individual circumstances.

WHEN TO INVEST

Determining the right time to invest can be challenging, as the financial markets are influenced by numerous factors and are inherently unpredictable. However, here are a few principles to consider when deciding when to invest:

Invest for the long term: Investing with a long-term perspective can help mitigate the impact of short-term market fluctuations. Time in the market is often more important than timing the market. By staying invested for an extended period, you can potentially benefit from the compounding growth of your investments.

Start early: The earlier you start investing, the more time your investments have to grow. Time is a powerful factor in building wealth due to the compounding effect, where your investment returns generate additional returns over time.

Have a financial plan: Before investing, it's essential to have a clear financial plan in place. Define your financial goals, such as saving for retirement, buying a home, or funding your children's education. Determine your risk tolerance, time horizon, and the amount of money you can comfortably invest. This will help you align your investments with your specific objectives.

Avoid timing the market: Trying to predict short-term market movements and investing based on market timing is notoriously difficult. It's challenging to consistently buy at the bottom and sell at the top. Instead, focus on the long-term trends and the fundamentals of the investments you are considering.

Dollar-cost averaging: Instead of investing a lump sum all at once, you can use a strategy called dollar-cost averaging. With this approach, you invest a fixed amount regularly, regardless of market conditions. This strategy can help reduce the impact of short-term market volatility and allow you to buy more shares when prices are low and fewer shares when prices are high.

Stay informed: Keep yourself informed about the latest financial news, market trends, and economic indicators. While you should avoid making impulsive investment decisions based on short-term market movements, having a general understanding of the investment landscape can help you make informed decisions.

Remember that investing always carries risks, and there will never be a perfect time to invest. It's crucial to assess your circumstances, goals, and risk tolerance before making investment decisions. Consider seeking guidance from a financial advisor who can provide personalized advice based on your specific situation.

WHO CAN INVEST

Generally, anyone with the financial means can invest. There are no specific restrictions on who can invest, but certain investment options may have specific requirements or limitations. Here are some categories of individuals who commonly invest:

Individuals: Most individual adults can invest their savings in various investment options. They can choose from a wide range of investment vehicles such as stocks, bonds, mutual funds, real estate, and more.

Minors: Minors can also invest, but they may require a custodian or guardian to manage the investments on their behalf. Special accounts, such as custodial accounts or trusts, can be set up to hold investments for minors until they reach the age of majority.

Retirement savers: Individuals planning for retirement can invest through retirement accounts such as 401(k)s, Individual Retirement Accounts (IRAs), or pension plans. These accounts offer tax advantages and are designed to help individuals save for their retirement years.

Business owners: Business owners can invest their capital in various ways, such as expanding their own business, investing in other businesses or startups, or diversifying their investments outside of their business ventures.

Institutional investors: Institutional investors include entities such as pension funds, insurance companies, endowments, foundations, and hedge funds. These entities pool together large amounts of capital and invest in a wide range of assets.

Non-profit organizations: Non-profit organizations may invest their funds to generate income or grow their endowments. They typically focus on investments that align with their mission and financial objectives.

Government entities: Governments at various levels, such as national, state, or local governments, may invest funds for various purposes, including infrastructure development, public pension funds, or sovereign wealth funds.

It's important to note that while anyone can invest, the specific investment options available may vary based on factors such as country of residence, regulatory requirements, and individual financial circumstances. It's always recommended to do thorough research, seeks professional advice when necessary, and understand the risks associated with any investment before committing your funds.

WHERE TO INVEST

Determining where to invest depends on various factors, including your financial goals, risk tolerance, time horizon, and knowledge about different investment options. Here are some common investment avenues to consider:

Stock market: Investing in individual stocks or exchange-traded funds (ETFs) allows you to participate in the ownership of publicly traded companies. Research and choose companies that align with your investment goals and consider factors like their financial health, growth potential, and industry trends.

Bonds: Bonds are debt instruments issued by governments, municipalities, or corporations. They offer fixed interest payments over a specified period, making them relatively less risky than stocks. Government bonds, corporate bonds, and municipal bonds are some options to explore.

Mutual funds and index funds: Mutual funds pool money from multiple investors to invest in a diversified portfolio of stocks, bonds, or other assets. Index funds, a type of mutual fund, aim to replicate the performance of a specific market index. These funds are managed by professionals and can offer broad market exposure.

Real estate: Investing in real estate can provide opportunities for rental income and potential appreciation. You can consider purchasing residential or commercial properties, real estate investment trusts (REITs), or real estate crowdfunding platforms.

Exchange-Traded Funds (ETFs): ETFs are investment funds that trade on stock exchanges. They provide exposure to a basket of assets like stocks, bonds, commodities, or sectors. ETFs offer diversification and flexibility, and they can be an efficient way to invest in specific areas of the market.

Retirement accounts: Contributing to retirement accounts such as 401(k)s or Individual Retirement Accounts (IRAs) provides tax advantages and helps build long-term wealth. These accounts offer a range of investment options, including stocks, bonds, mutual funds, and target-date funds.

Commodities: Investing in commodities such as gold, silver, oil, or agricultural products can provide diversification and act as a hedge against inflation. You can invest directly in physical commodities or through commodity futures contracts or exchange-traded products.

Peer-to-peer lending: Peer-to-peer lending platforms connect borrowers with individual lenders. By lending money to borrowers, you earn interest income. This investment option can provide higher returns compared to traditional savings accounts, but it also carries higher risks.

Startup investments: Investing in early-stage startups or venture capital funds can be an option for those looking for high-risk, high-reward opportunities. This avenue requires in-depth research and an understanding of the startup ecosystem.

Education and self-development: Investing in yourself through education, acquiring new skills, or professional certifications can also yield long-term benefits by enhancing your career prospects and income potential.

It's important to diversify your investments across different asset classes to manage risk effectively. Consider your investment goals, and risk tolerance, and seek professional advice when needed. Remember that investing involves risk, and it's crucial to do thorough research and understand the potential rewards and drawbacks of any investment before committing your funds.

WHERE NOT TO INVEST

While the investment landscape offers various opportunities, there are also areas where caution is warranted. Here are some areas where it is generally advised to proceed with caution or avoid investing altogether:

High-risk speculative investments: Investments that promise extraordinarily high returns with little to no risk often fall into the realm of speculation. These can include certain types of cryptocurrency investments, initial coin offerings (ICOs), penny stocks, and speculative derivatives. Such investments can be highly volatile, and illiquid, and may lack regulation or transparency.

Pyramid schemes and Ponzi schemes: Pyramid schemes and Ponzi schemes are fraudulent investment schemes that rely on new investors' funds to pay existing investors. These schemes eventually collapse when there are not enough new investors to sustain the payouts. Be wary of investments that promise guaranteed high returns with little effort or require you to recruit others into the scheme.

Unregulated or illegal investments: Investments that operate outside the bounds of regulatory oversight or are outright illegal should be avoided. This includes unregistered securities offerings, investment opportunities without proper documentation, or investments that involve illegal activities.

Get-rich-quick schemes: Investments that promise quick and substantial returns with little risk are typically too good to be true. Be skeptical of investments that rely on secret formulas, insider information, or proprietary trading systems that claim to generate extraordinary profits consistently.

High-cost and complex financial products: Some financial products come with high fees, commissions, or hidden charges that can eat into your returns. Additionally, complex financial products, such as leveraged derivatives or structured products, may be difficult to understand and carry a higher risk of losses.

Unfamiliar or highly speculative markets: Investing in unfamiliar markets or sectors without proper research and understanding can be risky. For example, investing in foreign markets with different economic and political conditions may carry additional risks. Speculative sectors like cryptocurrency or highly specialized industries should be approached with caution.

Debt-driven investments: Be cautious when considering investments that require excessive borrowing or margin trading. High levels of debt can amplify losses and pose significant risks, especially if market conditions deteriorate.

Individual company stocks without proper research: Investing in individual company stocks without conducting thorough research can expose you to specific company risks. Lack of diversification and reliance on a single company's performance can be risky. It is important to understand a company's financials, competitive position, and industry dynamics before investing.

Emotional or impulsive investments: Making investment decisions based on emotions, market hype, or short-term trends can lead to poor outcomes. Avoid making impulsive investment decisions without proper analysis and a well-defined investment strategy.

Investments without due diligence: Always conduct thorough due diligence and research before investing. Avoid investments that lack transparent information, have questionable management teams, or lack a clear and compelling business proposition.

Remember that investing involves risks, and it's important to carefully assess any investment opportunity before committing your funds. If you have doubts or lack the necessary expertise, consider consulting with a financial advisor or professional who can provide guidance tailored to your specific situation.

WHO TO MANAGE INVESTMENT

There are various options available for managing investments, depending on your preferences, knowledge, and the complexity of your investment strategy. Here are some common approaches to consider:

Self-management: Managing your investments on your own can be a cost-effective option if you have the knowledge, time, and confidence to make informed investment decisions. This approach requires conducting thorough research, staying informed about market trends, and actively monitoring and rebalancing your portfolio.

Financial advisors: Working with a professional financial advisor can provide expertise and guidance in managing your investments. Financial advisors can help you develop an investment plan tailored to your goals and risk tolerance, provide ongoing portfolio management, and offer advice on asset allocation, investment selection, and risk management.

Robo-advisors: Robo-advisors are digital platforms that use algorithms to provide automated investment management services. They typically use questionnaires to assess your risk profile and investment goals and then create and manage a diversified portfolio of exchange-traded funds (ETFs) based on your preferences. Robo-advisors can be a cost-effective option for investors looking for automated, low-cost portfolio management.

Mutual fund managers: Investing in mutual funds allows you to benefit from professional fund managers who oversee the portfolio and make investment decisions on behalf of the fund's investors. Mutual fund managers conduct research, select securities, and manage the fund's holdings according to the fund's investment objectives.

Institutional investment managers: Institutional investors, such as pension funds, endowments, or insurance companies, often have in-house investment teams or outsource investment management to professional asset management firms. These managers handle large pools of funds and employ investment strategies tailored to meet specific investment goals.

Family office: High-net-worth individuals or families may establish their own family office, which is a dedicated team of professionals who manage the family's investments, financial affairs, and wealth planning. Family offices provide comprehensive investment management services customized to the family's specific needs and objectives.

It's important to consider your level of investment knowledge, the complexity of your investment needs, and the time you can dedicate to managing your investments when deciding who will manage your investments. Additionally, be sure to evaluate the qualifications, track record, and fees associated with any professional you consider working with.

Regardless of the approach you choose, staying informed, regularly reviewing your investments, and reassessing your financial goals and risk tolerance are important components of successful investment management.

WHO TO PARTNER WITH IN INVESTMENT

When considering partnership opportunities in investment, there are several entities or professionals you can potentially collaborate with. The choice depends on your specific investment needs, goals, and the level of involvement you desire. Here are some potential partners to consider:

Financial advisors: Working with a financial advisor can provide personalized guidance and expertise in developing an investment strategy aligned with your goals and risk tolerance. They can offer recommendations, monitor your investments, and provide ongoing advice to help you make informed decisions.

Investment managers: Investment management firms or professionals specialize in managing investment portfolios on behalf of individuals or institutions. They have expertise in various asset classes and can handle the day-to-day management of your investments, ensuring they align with your investment objectives.

Real estate agents or brokers: If you're interested in investing in real estate, partnering with a knowledgeable real estate agent or broker can provide access to potential investment properties, market insights, and assistance in negotiating deals. They can help you find suitable properties and navigate the intricacies of real estate transactions.

Venture capitalists or angel investors: If you're considering investing in startups or early-stage companies, partnering with venture capitalists or angel investors can provide access to investment opportunities, industry expertise, and networks. They often invest in promising startups and provide mentorship and guidance to entrepreneurs.

Private equity firms: Private equity firms invest in privately-held companies and can partner with you to pool capital and invest in larger-scale projects or acquisitions. They can provide expertise in managing and growing businesses, along with access to a network of industry contacts.

Peer networks or investment groups: Joining investment clubs, online communities, or networking groups can provide opportunities to collaborate with like-minded individuals interested in investing. These networks facilitate knowledge sharing, idea generation, and potential co-investment opportunities.

Financial institutions: Banks, brokerage firms, or investment platforms may offer investment services and products. Partnering with reputable financial institutions can provide access to a wide range of investment options, research, and investment tools.

Legal and tax professionals: Consulting with legal and tax professionals is crucial to ensure compliance, understand the legal framework of investment transactions, and optimize your tax strategy. They can guide you on structuring investments, tax planning, and potential legal considerations.

Business partners or co-investors: Forming partnerships or co-investing with individuals who share similar investment goals can provide opportunities to pool resources, share expertise, and spread risk. This can be particularly beneficial for larger-scale investments or projects.

When seeking an investment partner, it's important to evaluate their qualifications, track record, reputation, and alignment with your investment objectives. Additionally, consider the terms of the partnership, including roles, responsibilities, and any potential fees or profit-sharing arrangements.

Note that partnering with professionals or entities does not guarantee investment success, and it's important to conduct due diligence, perform thorough research, and make informed decisions based on your financial circumstances and risk tolerance.

RISKS ASSOCIATED WITH INVESTMENT

Investing comes with various risks that investors should be aware of. Understanding these risks can help you make informed investment decisions. Here are some common risks associated with investments:

Market risk: Market risk refers to the possibility of your investments losing value due to general market fluctuations. Factors such as economic conditions, geopolitical events, interest rates, and investor sentiment can impact the overall market and the performance of your investments.

Volatility risk: Volatility risk is the potential for significant price fluctuations in your investments. Investments with higher volatility, such as stocks or certain types of cryptocurrencies, can experience rapid price swings, potentially leading to significant gains or losses.

Credit risk: Credit risk is the risk that a borrower, such as a company or government, may default on their debt obligations. If you invest in bonds or lend money to entities, there is a possibility of a non-payment or delayed payment of interest or principal.

Inflation risk: Inflation risk refers to the potential for the purchasing power of your investments to be eroded over time due to rising inflation. Inflation can reduce the real value of your returns, especially if the returns on your investments do not outpace inflation.

Liquidity risk: Liquidity risk relates to the ease with which you can buy or sell an investment. Some investments, such as real estate or certain types of private equity, can be relatively illiquid, meaning it may be challenging to sell them quickly without incurring significant costs or delays.

Concentration risk: Concentration risk arises from having a significant portion of your portfolio invested in a single asset, sector, or geographic region. If that specific investment or sector performs poorly, it can have a disproportionate impact on your overall portfolio.

Political and regulatory risk: Political and regulatory changes can impact the investment landscape. Government policies, new regulations, or leadership changes can introduce uncertainties and potentially affect specific industries or investments.

Currency risk: Currency risk arises when investing in foreign assets denominated in a different currency. Fluctuations in exchange rates can affect the value of your investments when converting them back to your home currency.

Interest rate risk: Interest rate risk is the risk that changes in interest rates can affect the value of fixed-income investments, such as bonds. When interest rates rise, bond prices typically fall, and vice versa.

Operational and counterparty risk: Operational risk refers to the risk of loss resulting from operational failures, errors, or disruptions within financial institutions or investment platforms. Counterparty risk is the risk that the party on the other side of a transaction, such as a brokerage or financial institution, fails to fulfill its obligations.

It's important to note that different investments carry different levels of risk. Higher-risk investments often have the potential for higher returns but also come with increased volatility and potential losses. Before investing, carefully consider your risk tolerance, investment objectives, and the specific risks associated with the investment you are considering. Diversification, thorough research, and staying informed can help mitigate some of these risks. Additionally, consulting with a financial advisor can provide personalized guidance tailored to your specific circumstances.

HOW TO SAFEGUARD YOUR INVESTMENT

Safeguarding your investments is essential to protect your capital and mitigate risks. Here are some key steps to help safeguard your investments:

Diversify your portfolio: Diversification is the practice of spreading your investments across different asset classes, industries, and regions. By diversifying, you reduce the impact of any single investment or market downturn on your overall portfolio. Diversification helps to balance risk and potential returns.

Set clear investment goals and risk tolerance: Establish clear investment goals and define your risk tolerance. Having a well-defined investment plan aligned with your goals and risk tolerance will help you make informed decisions and avoid impulsive actions based on short-term market fluctuations.

Perform thorough research: Before investing in any asset, conduct thorough research. Understand the fundamentals of the investment, including its historical performance, market trends, financial health, and the risks associated with it. Research can help you make more informed investment decisions and avoid potential pitfalls.

Stay informed: Stay up to date with market news, economic trends, and any relevant developments that may impact your investments. Be aware of factors that could influence the performance of your investments, such as changes in regulations, industry trends, or geopolitical events. Regularly review your investment holdings and performance reports.

Regularly review and rebalance your portfolio: Periodically review your investment portfolio to ensure it remains aligned with your goals and risk tolerance. Rebalance your portfolio by adjusting the allocation of your investments if they deviate from your desired asset allocation. This helps maintain a diversified and balanced portfolio.

Avoid market timing and emotional decision-making: Trying to time the market or making investment decisions based on emotions can be risky. Instead, focus on a long-term investment strategy and avoid succumbing to short-term market fluctuations. Stick to your investment plan and avoid making impulsive decisions based on fear or greed.

Understand fees and costs: Be aware of the fees and costs associated with your investments. High fees can eat into your returns over time. Evaluate the fees charged by investment platforms, funds, or advisors, and consider lower-cost alternatives when appropriate.

Monitor investment performance and statements: Regularly review your investment performance and account statements. Check for any discrepancies, errors, or unauthorized transactions. Promptly address any issues with your investment provider or broker.

Consider professional advice: If you are uncertain or lack the expertise to manage your investments, consider seeking professional advice from a qualified financial advisor. They can provide guidance, monitor your investments, and help you make informed decisions aligned with your financial goals.

Stay vigilant against fraud: Be cautious of investment scams and fraudulent schemes. Protect your personal and financial information, and only invest with reputable institutions or professionals. Be skeptical of investment opportunities that promise unrealistic returns or pressure you to make quick decisions.

Remember, investing involves risks, and it's essential to assess and manage those risks effectively. By following these steps and staying informed, you can help safeguard your investments and increase the likelihood of achieving your financial objectives.

20 LAWS OF INVESTMENT

While there is no definitive list of "laws" of investment, there are several principles and guidelines that are commonly followed by successful investors. Here are 20 general principles that can help guide your investment decisions:

Diversify your portfolio to spread risk across different asset classes, industries, and geographic regions.

Invest for the long term to benefit from compounding growth and ride out short-term market fluctuations.

Understand the concept of risk and return: Higher potential returns typically come with higher levels of risk.

Conduct thorough research before investing in any asset or company.

Develop a clear investment strategy based on your financial goals, risk tolerance, and time horizon.

Don't invest in something you don't understand. Avoid speculative investments without proper knowledge.

Keep emotions in check and avoid making impulsive investment decisions based on short-term market movements.

Focus on the fundamentals of the investments you consider, such as earnings, cash flow, and valuation.

Regularly review and monitor your investments, but avoid overtrading or making frequent changes based on market noise.

Consider the impact of fees and expenses on your investment returns and choose low-cost investment options when possible.

Have an emergency fund in place to cover unexpected expenses and avoid selling investments at unfavorable times.

Stay informed about market trends, economic indicators, and changes in regulations that may affect your investments.

Be patient and avoid chasing short-term market trends or trying to time the market.

Don't put all your eggs in one basket. Spread your investments across different assets to reduce risk.

Avoid taking on excessive debt to invest. Maintain a healthy balance between your investment capital and debt levels.

Consider the impact of taxes on your investment returns and explore tax-efficient investment strategies.

Learn from your investment mistakes and adjust your approach based on past experiences.

Stay disciplined and stick to your investment plan, even during periods of market volatility.

Take a long-term perspective when evaluating the performance of your investments, rather than focusing on short-term fluctuations.

Consider seeking professional advice from a financial advisor if you need assistance with investment decisions or managing your portfolio.

Remember that investing involves risks, and these principles should be considered as general guidelines rather than rigid rules. Your investment decisions should be based on your circumstances, goals, and risk tolerance.

HOW TO PLAN INVESTMENT

Planning your investments is a crucial step in achieving your financial goals. Here are some key steps to help you plan your investment strategy:

Set your financial goals: Define your short-term and long-term financial goals. Are you saving for retirement, buying a house, funding your child's education, or building wealth? Clearly articulating your goals will help shape your investment plan.

Assess your risk tolerance: Understand your risk tolerance by evaluating how comfortable you are with the potential ups and downs of investment returns. Consider your financial situation, time horizon, and emotional capacity to handle market volatility. This assessment will help determine the appropriate asset allocation and investment choices.

Determine your investment time horizon: Identify the timeframe over which you plan to achieve your financial goals. Short-term goals, such as saving for a down payment on a house, may require more conservative investments, while long-term goals, like retirement, can tolerate more risk and potentially benefit from higher-return investments.

Determine your investment capital: Assess how much money you can allocate towards investments. Consider your current financial situation, income, expenses, and any outstanding debts. It's important to strike a balance between investing and maintaining an adequate emergency fund for unexpected expenses.

Educate yourself: Take the time to educate yourself about different investment options, asset classes, and investment strategies. Understand the risks and potential returns associated with each investment option. Consider reading books, taking online courses, or consulting with a financial advisor to enhance your investment knowledge.

Define your asset allocation: Asset allocation refers to the distribution of your investment capital across different asset classes, such as stocks, bonds, real estate, or cash. It is a critical decision that determines the risk and returns potential of your portfolio. Allocate your investments based on your risk tolerance, goals, and time horizon.

Select specific investments: Once you have determined your asset allocation, research and select specific investments within each asset class. Consider factors such as historical performance, fees, diversification, the quality of the investment, and the track record of the investment manager. Diversify your investments across different industries and regions to spread risk.

Monitor and review your investments: Regularly review your investment portfolio to ensure it remains aligned with your goals and risk tolerance. Monitor the performance of your investments, stay informed about market trends, and assess the need for rebalancing your portfolio to maintain the desired asset allocation.

Stay disciplined and avoid emotional decision-making: Investment markets can be volatile, and emotions can lead to poor investment decisions. Develop a disciplined investment approach based on your plan and long-term goals. Avoid making impulsive changes based on short-term market fluctuations.

Seek professional advice if needed: If you are uncertain or lack the time and expertise to manage your investments, consider consulting with a financial advisor. They can provide personalized guidance, help you develop an investment plan, and assist in selecting suitable investments based on your goals and risk profile.

Remember, investment planning is a dynamic process. Regularly revisit and update your investment plan as your goals, financial situation, or market conditions change. It's important to review and adjust your investments as needed to stay on track toward achieving your financial objectives.

HOW TO SOURCE FOR CAPITAL FOR INVESTMENT

Sourcing capital for investment can be done through various avenues. Here are some common methods to consider:

Personal savings: One of the most straightforward ways to source capital for investment is through your savings. By setting aside a portion of your income over time, you can accumulate funds to invest.

Investment income: If you already have investments generating income, you can reinvest those earnings back into your portfolio. Dividends from stocks, interest from bonds, or rental income from real estate can be used to fund additional investments.

Budgeting and expense management: Review your budget and identify areas where you can reduce expenses or increase savings. By optimizing your spending habits, you can free up more funds to allocate towards investments.

Selling assets: Consider selling assets you no longer need or that have appreciated. This could include selling unused property, vehicles, collectibles, or other valuable possessions to generate capital for investment.

Loan or mortgage: If you are comfortable taking on debt, you can explore options like personal loans or leveraging the equity in your home through a mortgage or home equity line of credit (HELOC). However, it's important to carefully consider the risks and costs associated with borrowing.

Crowdfunding or peer-to-peer lending: Online platforms provide opportunities to raise capital from a large number of individuals through crowdfunding or peer-to-peer lending. These platforms connect investors with borrowers or entrepreneurs seeking funding for specific projects or ventures.

Family and friends: You can consider approaching family members or close friends who may be interested in investing or providing a loan. However, when involving personal relationships in financial matters, it's crucial to establish clear terms and agreements to avoid potential conflicts.

Angel investors or venture capitalists: If you have a business idea or startup, you can seek capital from angel investors or venture capitalists. These individuals or firms specialize in providing funding to early-stage companies in exchange for an equity stake.

Government programs and grants: Investigate government programs or grants that may be available to support specific types of investments, such as renewable energy projects, research and development initiatives, or small business ventures.

Retirement funds: Depending on your country's regulations, you may have the option to tap into retirement savings, such as a 401(k) or IRA, through methods like a loan or a hardship withdrawal. However, be mindful of the potential tax implications and the impact on your long-term retirement savings.

Remember to carefully evaluate the costs, risks, and terms associated with each capital source before making a decision. It's important to assess your financial situation, consider your risk tolerance, and ensure that the capital source aligns with your investment goals and strategy. Consulting with a financial advisor can provide further guidance on the most suitable options for sourcing capital based on your specific circumstances.

31 SECTORS TO TRY INVESTMENT
Here is a list of 30 sectors that you could consider for investment purposes:

1 Technology and Software
2 Healthcare and Pharmaceuticals
3 Financial Services and Banking
4 Renewable Energy
5 E-commerce and Online Retail
6 Telecommunications
7 Artificial Intelligence and Machine Learning
8 Electric Vehicles and Clean
9 Transportation
10 Consumer Goods and Retail
11 Biotechnology
12 Real Estate and Property Development
13 Cybersecurity
14 Aerospace and Defense
15 Robotics and Automation
16 Sustainable Agriculture

17 Entertainment and Media

18 Education Technology

19 Water and Environmental Services

20 Infrastructure and Construction

21 Gaming and Esports

22 Internet of Things (IoT)

23 Renewable Fuels

24 Logistics and Supply Chain

25 Clean Energy Technology

26 Fintech (Financial Technology)

27 HealthTech

28 Smart Cities

29 Insurance

30 Travel and Tourism

31 Nanotechnology

Please note that this list is not exhaustive, and the performance and prospects of each sector can vary over time. It's essential to conduct thorough research, assess market conditions, and consider your investment objectives and risk tolerance when selecting sectors to invest in. Additionally, consulting with a financial advisor can provide personalized advice based on your specific circumstances and investment goals.